If you are reading this book, know that you are special.

Red Bear Flamin' Hots are the best snacks ever. I eat them every single day.

I eat them for breakfast.

I eat them for lunch.

I would love to eat flamin' hots for dinner, but my dad makes me eat green peas, carrots and broccoli, yuck!

Flamin' hots are too hot for my dad.

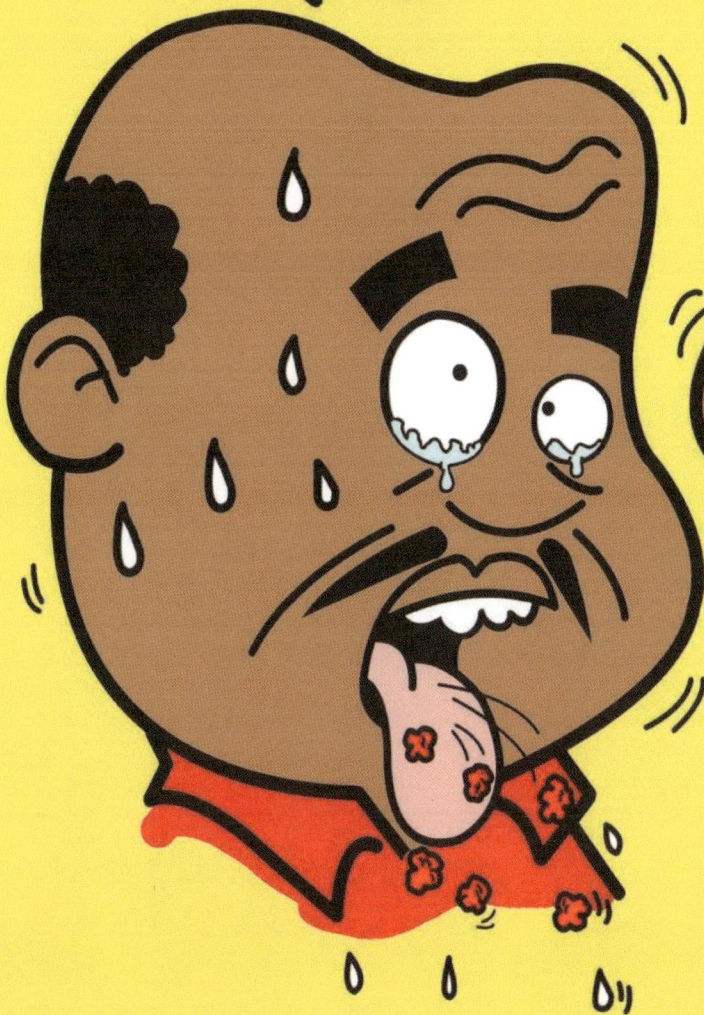

Flamin' hots are also too hot for my cat Rico.

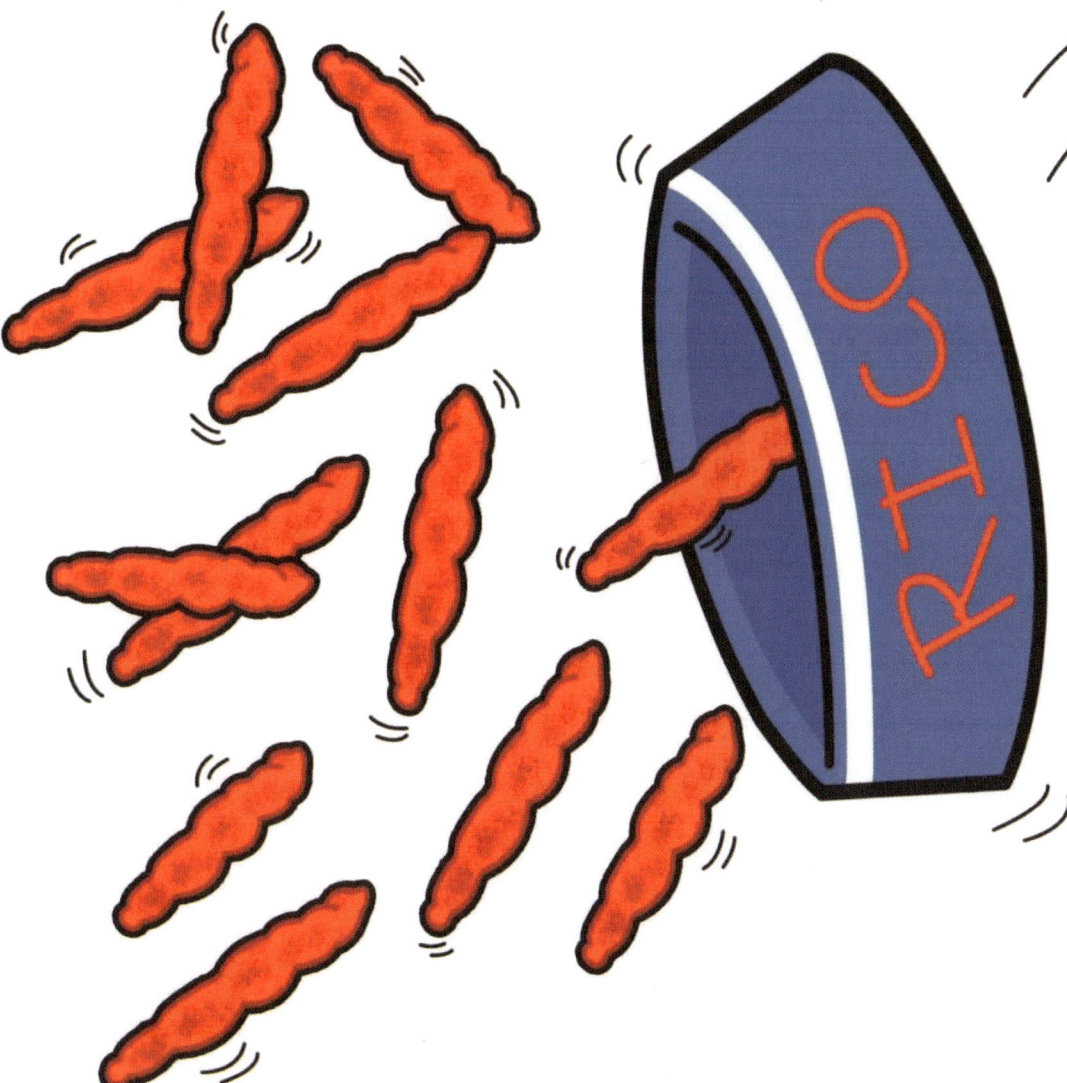

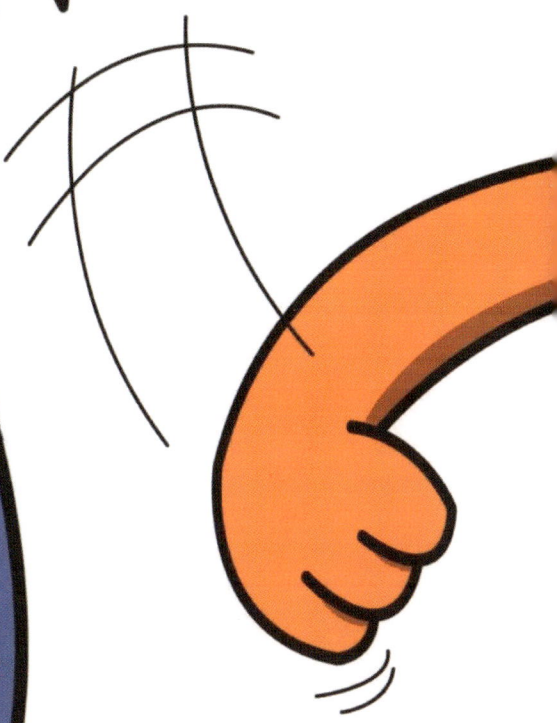

After dinner, I brush my teeth with flamin' hots toothpaste.

Before I go to bed, I take a nice, flamin' hot shower.

One day I threw my airplane
and broke my dad's trophy.

1st PLACE

PIZZA EATING CONTEST

BEFORE

AFTER

Later on that day, my dad asked, "Germaine, did you break my trophy?"

"Nope," I said, "I never touched it. Maybe it broke by itself."

Somehow, my dad knew I was lying. He took my flamin' hots and sent me to my room.

After sitting in my room for awhile, I felt bad about breaking my dad's trophy and lying to him. I should have been honest.

My dad was on the couch watching a movie.
"Dad," I said, "Can we talk?"
My dad turned off the t.v. and said, "Sure, Germaine."

"Ok, well dad, I am sorry for breaking your trophy and lying to you. I was afraid that I would get into trouble. Can you please forgive me?"

My dad smiled and said, "Yes, Germaine, I forgive you. Thanks for being honest, ok?"

"Ok dad."

"Germaine," my dad said.
"Yes dad?"
"I think these belong to you."

Thanks Dad!

Made in the USA
Columbia, SC
20 May 2018